I REMEMBER BEIRUT

STORY AND ART BY ZEINA ABIRACHED
TRANSLATION BY EDWARD GAUVIN

FIRST AMERICAN EDITION PUBLISHED IN 2014 BY GRAPHIC UNIVERSE™.
PUBLISHED BY ARRANGEMENT WITH ÉDITIONS CAMBOURAKIS.

I REMEMBER BEIRUT
©2008 ÉDITIONS CAMBOURAKIS
ENGLISH TRANSLATION COPYRIGHT ©2014 BY LERNER PUBLISHING GROUP, INC.

MAP ON PAGE 5 ©LAURA WESTLUND/INDEPENDENT PICTURE SERVICE.

GRAPHIC UNIVERSE™ IS A TRADEMARK OF LERNER PUBLISHING GROUP, INC.

GRAPHIC UNIVERSE™
A DIVISION OF LERNER PUBLISHING GROUP, INC.
241 FIRST AVENUE NORTH
MINNEAPOLIS, MN 55401 USA

FOR READING LEVELS AND MORE INFORMATION, LOOK UP THIS TITLE AT
WWW.LERNERBOOKS.COM.

LIBRARY OF CONGRESS CATALOGING-IN-PUBLICATION DATA
ABIRACHED, ZEINA, 1981-
     I REMEMBER BEIRUT / WRITTEN BY ZEINA ABIRACHED ; ART BY ZEINA ABIRACHED ;
TRANSLATION BY EDWARD GAUVIN.
     P.   CM
   ISBN 978-1-4677-3822-4 (LIB. BDG. : ALK. PAPER)
   ISBN 978-1-4677-4660-1 (EB PDF)
   1. ABIRACHED, ZEINA, 1981-—JUVENILE LITERATURE. 2. BEIRUT (LEBANON)—
BIOGRAPHY—JUVENILE LITERATURE. 3. LEBANON—HISTORY—20TH CENTURY—JUVENILE
LITERATURE. 4. ABIRACHED, ZEINA, 1981-—COMIC BOOKS, STRIPS, ETC. 5. BEIRUT
(LEBANON)—BIOGRAPHY—COMIC BOOKS, STRIPS, ETC. 6. LEBANON—HISTORY—20TH
CENTURY—COMIC BOOKS, STRIPS, ETC. 7. GRAPHIC NOVELS. I. TITLE.
DS87.2.A333A3 2014
741.5'95692—DC23   2013047112

MANUFACTURED IN THE UNITED STATES OF AMERICA
2 - PC - 1/1/15

I REMEMBER BEIRUT

ZEINA ABIRACHED

GRAPHIC UNIVERSE™ • MINNEAPOLIS

INTRODUCTION

The Lebanese Civil War lasted from 1975 to 1990. The conflict
began when fighting broke out between the Christians of Lebanon
and an alliance of Lebanese Muslims and Palestinian refugees.
Over time, some groups of Christian and Muslim combatants
also began to fight among themselves. Multiple outside countries
became involved in efforts to restore order. For many years, the
fighting divided Lebanon's capital city, Beirut. Zeina Abirached
was born in the middle of the civil war, in 1981.

LEBANON AND SURROUNDING AREA 1975–1990

HOMS •

TRIPOLI

MEDITERRANEAN SEA

N

LEBANON

SYRIA

BEIRUT

AREA OF INSET

SIDON •

DAMASCUS
★

TYRE •

INTERNATIONAL BORDER
DISPUTED BORDER
CITY BORDER (INSET)
★ CAPITAL
• CITY

MILES
0   10   20   30
0   20   40
KILOMETERS

TEL AVIV •

ISRAEL

BEIRUT, LEBANON

WEST BEIRUT (MUSLIM)

EAST BEIRUT (CHRISTIAN)

DEMARCATION LINE ("GREEN LINE")

0   .5   1   1.5 MILES
0   1   2 KILOMETERS

JERUSALEM •

"NOThING DISTINGUISHES
MEMORIES FROM ORDINARY
MOMENTS. ONLY LATER DO
THEY MAKE THEMSELVES
KNOWN, FROM THEIR SCARS."

—CHRIS MARKER

I REMEMBER MY MOTHER'S NAVY BLUE RENAULT 12.

I REMEMBER THE SIDES WERE RIDDLED WITH BULLETS. EVERY TIME A SHELL HIT IN THE NEIGHBORHOOD, THE WINDSHIELD WOULD SHATTER.

RUE 60 | ٦٠. شارع

شارع يوسف سمعاني
RUE YOUSSEF SEMAANI

I REMEMBER THAT AFTER A WHILE, MY MOTHER GOT SICK OF REPLACING THE WINDSHIELD ON HER R12. SHE WOULD WEAR SUNGLASSES WHEN SHE DROVE, TO SHIELD HER EYES.

I REMEMBER THAT DURING THE WAR, THE SCHOOL BUS SKIPPED OUR NEIGHBORHOOD. THE NEIGHBORHOOD'S ALLEYS WERE CLOSE TO THE DEMARCATION LINE AND HAD A DANGEROUS REPUTATION.

TO WEST BEIRUT

TO WARD'S

HOME

WHERE NO MAN'S LAND ACTUALLY STARTS

WHERE PEOPLE THINK NO MAN'S LAND STARTS

THE BUS WOULD STOP AT WARD'S ICE CREAM PARLOR AT 6:30 EVERY MORNING AND 3:30 EVERY AFTERNOON.

BY VIRTUE OF BEING ON THE EDGE OF THE ZONE WHERE THE BUS DIDN'T DARE GO, WARD'S HAD BEEN TURNED INTO A BUS STOP.

AT FIRST, THE PARENTS IN OUR NEIGHBORHOOD TOOK TURNS DRIVING KIDS TO WARD'S IN THE MORNING AND PICKING THEM UP IN THE AFTERNOON.

THEN THEY ENTRUSTED THIS THANKLESS TASK TO MR. GEORGE.

MR. GEORGE WAS A TAXI DRIVER. HE HAD A HUGE CAR EVERYONE CALLED "THE BOAT." HE ALWAYS PARKED IT AT THE INTERSECTION OF LEBANON STREET AND ST. JOSEPH UNIVERSITY STREET. WE COULD ALWAYS FIND HIM STANDING NEXT TO THE CAR, LOOKING FOR HIS NEXT FARE.

HELLO!

WELCOME!

HOW'S IT GOING?

HOW'S YOUR HEALTH?

YOUR FAMILY?

INSHA'ALLAH!

FOURTEEN YEARS LATER, HE TAUGHT ME TO DRIVE ON THE STREETS OF BEIRUT, JUST BEFORE I GOT MY LICENSE.

his right foot braking instinctively

SLOW DOWN!

SLOW DOWN!

YEE-HAW!

I REMEMBER THAT MR. GEORGE'S LOVE FOR HIS CAR KNEW NO END.

HE POLISHED IT ADORINGLY EVERY MORNING.

(EVEN THOUGH WE HADN'T HAD RUNNING WATER SINCE THE WAR STARTED.)

I ALSO REMEMBER HE HAD A REALLY LONG FINGERNAIL ON HIS LEFT PINKY (SUPPOSEDLY A SIGN OF MANLINESS).

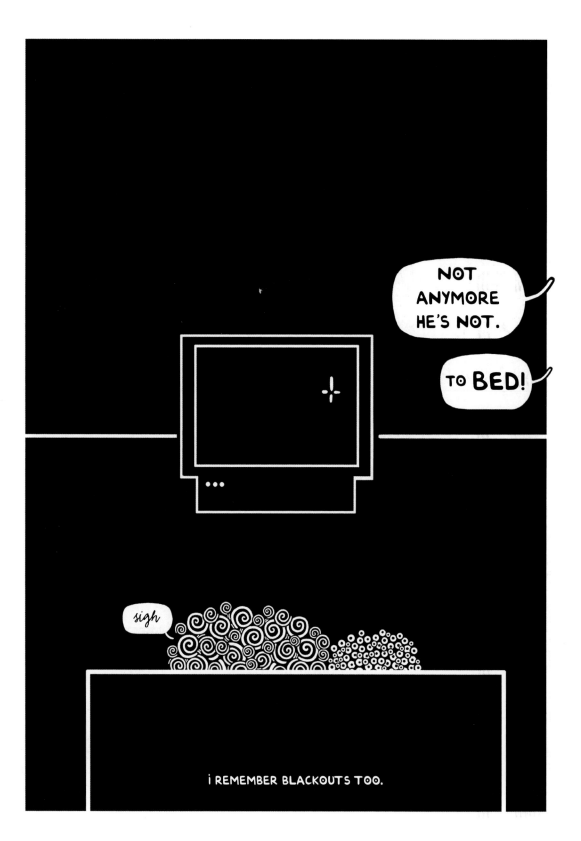

I REMEMBER WHEN THERE WAS NO ELECTRICITY OR GAS, WE USED KEROSENE FOR HEATING.

THE GAS MAN WOULD ROAM THE NEIGHBORHOOD WITH A TANK ON A LITTLE HORSE-DRAWN CART.

i REMEMBER IT WAS HARD TO FIND CERTAIN ITEMS IN THE SUPERMARKET.
AND THAT COCA-COLA HADN'T HIT LEBANON YET.

I REMEMBER TAPES...

TCHiC
TCHiC
TCHiCKi
TCHiC
TCHiC

AND THE SOUND THEY MADE WHEN YOU SHOOK THEM.

I REMEMBER THAT DURING THE WAR, MY FATHER GOT INTO THE HABIT OF CRANKING UP THE VOLUME ON HIS MUSIC.

Berlioz's Grand
Funeral and
Triumphal Symphony

i REMEMBER ASSUMING THAT HE CRANKED UP THE VOLUME iN ORDER TO DROWN
OUT THE CHAOS OUTSIDE.

BUT WHEN THE WAR GREW QUIET, HE KEPT CRANKING THE VOLUME UP.

AND I REMEMBER THAT THE NEIGHBORS BEGAN TO COMPLAIN.

SO HE BOUGHT A PAIR OF HEADPHONES.

i REMEMBER THE NIGHT OF JANUARY 27, 1989.

LINE UP!

THAT MORNING, MR. GEORGE HAD DROPPED US OFF AT WARD'S, WHERE WE'D BOARDED THE BUS FOR SCHOOL. AS USUAL.

WAAAAAAH!

i WANT TO SEE A STRAIGHT LINE!

ONCE WE WERE IN THE GYM, OUR TEACHERS PASSED OUT WATER AND CHEESE SANDWICHES.

AND SOLDIERS IN THE BARRACKS NEXT DOOR LENT US SLEEPING BAGS FOR THE NIGHT.

I REMEMBER REALIZING OUR TEACHERS WERE AS SCARED AS WE WERE.

I REMEMBER GLIMPSING, IN A CORNER OF THE GYM, THE TIPS OF THEIR CIGARETTES GLOWING IN THE DARK.

I DON'T REMEMBER WHAT HAPPENED NEXT, SINCE I FINALLY GOT PUNISHED. I SPENT THE REST OF THE NIGHT LOCKED UP IN THE GYM BATHROOM.

WELL...

MAYBE NOT ALL NIGHT.

BUT IT SEEMED LIKE A VERY LONG TIME.

THE NEXT MORNING, MY MOTHER AND CHUCRI CAME TO GET US IN THE R12.

my darlings

I REMEMBER SEEING ROADBLOCKS MADE FROM BURNT-OUT CITY BUSES ON THE RIDE BACK. I REMEMBER THEY WERE BERLIET BRAND BUSES.

TWO DAYS LATER, WE CELEBRATED MY MOTHER'S BIRTHDAY.
ANHALA MADE A CHOCOLATE CAKE.

* A POPULAR BIRTHDAY SONG

AS FOR US: WE WERE ON VACATION.

I REMEMBER THAT I HAD TAKEN TO LEAVING MY BACKPACK BY MY BED AT NIGHT.

KLIK!

A NOTEBOOK

A LITTLE RAY-O-VAC FLASHLIGHT

A PENCIL

BATTERIES

MY *TINTIN: RED RACKHAM'S TREASURE* COMIC

PHOTOS

MY WALKMAN

MY STUFFED PUPPY

MY *RUBBER SOUL* BEATLES TAPE

CHICLETS CHEWING GUM (YELLOW)

MY *JONATHAN LIVINGSTON SEAGULL* BOOK

IN MY BACKPACK, I HAD EVERYTHING I WANTED TO TAKE WITH ME, IF WE HAD TO RUN.

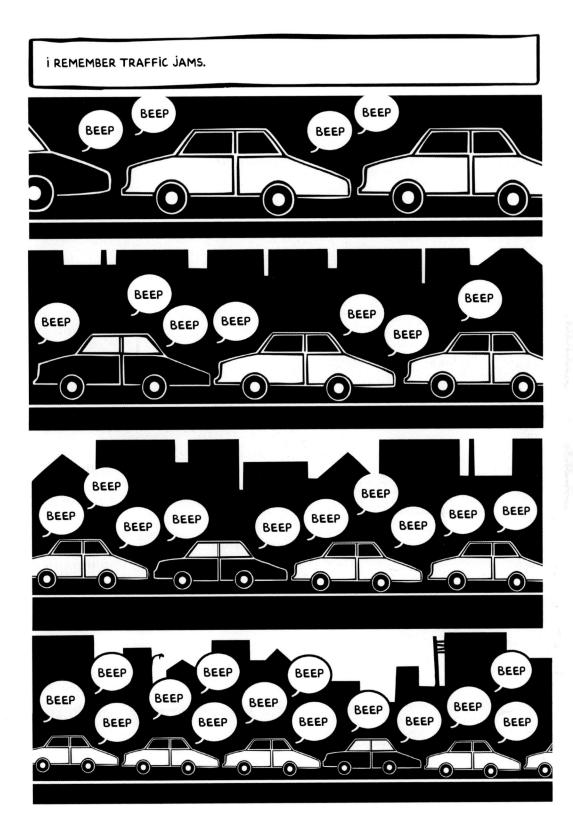

DURING THE WAR, MANY ROADS LINKING BEIRUT TO THE REST OF THE NATION WERE SHUT DOWN.

the R12

TRYING TO GET OUT OF THE CITY COULD TAKE FIVE HOURS...

FOUR OF THEM AT A STANDSTILL.

I REMEMBER ALL THE THINGS MY MOTHER HAD IN THE CAR: WATER, FRUIT JUICE, SANDWICHES, CANDY, TISSUES, PILLOWS, BLANKETS, PLAYING CARDS, AND A BOOK OF RIDDLES...

I REMEMBER THE BOAT WE TOOK IN 1989 TO GO TO CYPRUS.

THAT YEAR, LOTS OF LEBANESE TOOK REFUGE IN LARNACA, A FEW HOURS BY BOAT FROM THE PORT OF JOUNIEH.

I REMEMBER I WAS CARRYING MY BACKPACK.

I REMEMBER THAT EVERY LIVING ROOM HAD A PLATTER WITH PACKS OF CIGARETTES ON IT.

THE HOSTESS WOULD OFFER THEM TO HER GUESTS, AS IF SHE WERE PASSING AROUND CHOCOLATES.

I REMEMBER THE YEAR I HAD TO GET BRACES.

THAT SAME YEAR, I FOUND OUT I WAS NEARSIGHTED...

AND I THOUGHT IT WOULD BE A GOOD IDEA TO GET MY HAIR CUT.

NOT EXACTLY CAUSE FOR CELEBRATION.

I REMEMBER THAT AT THE BEGINNING OF THE WAR, A SHELL DESTROYED THE WALL BETWEEN THE TWO SALONS.

NOW A SINGLE SPACE, THE TWO HAIR SALONS BECAME A PEDESTRIAN THOROUGHFARE.

PEOPLE FROM THE NEIGHBORHOOD USED THE GAP IN ORDER TO STAY OFF THE SIDEWALK. AT THE TIME, LEBANON STREET WAS EXPOSED TO SNIPER FIRE.

AFTER THE WAR, THE WALL WAS REBUILT.

LOCALS STARTED USING THE SIDEWALK AGAIN.

SALON SI BELLE — FOR LADIES

SALON FOUAD — FOR MEN

AND I WOULD TRY TO SNEAK BY THE SALON SI BELLE WITHOUT GETTING NOTICED.

i REMEMBER OLD KIT KAT WRAPPERS.

I REMEMBER THE FIRST TIME I WENT TO WEST BEIRUT. IT WAS 1989, WHEN THE WAR HAD MOVED EAST. IN THE WEST, LIFE WAS BACK TO NORMAL.

I REMEMBER THE OLD LIGHTHOUSE.

I REMEMBER THE FERRIS WHEEL.

I REMEMBER PEOPLE ALL OVER THE STREETS.

I REMEMBER THE BEACH AT RAMLET AL-BAIDA.

I REMEMBER THE SEA.

BUT I REMEMBER MY SURPRISE WHEN, TEN YEARS AFTER THE WAR ENDED, I WAS WALKING IN BEIRUT AND REALIZED THAT THE STREET ACROSS FROM WHERE I LIVED, WHICH FOR FIFTEEN YEARS HAD BEEN THE "OTHER SIDE," WAS ALSO CALLED... YOUSSEF SEMAANI STREET.

MOM, IS DOWNTOWN FAR?

WHY, NO!

LOOK, IT'S RIGHT ACROSS THE STREET.

COMING?

LET'S GO!

DID YOU TIE YOUR SHOES ALL BY YOURSELF?

YES!

DOWNTOWN HAD BEEN THE SCENE OF VIOLENT FIGHTING, BUT IT WAS ACCESSIBLE ONCE MORE TO THE PEOPLE OF BEIRUT.

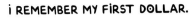
I REMEMBER MY FIRST DOLLAR.

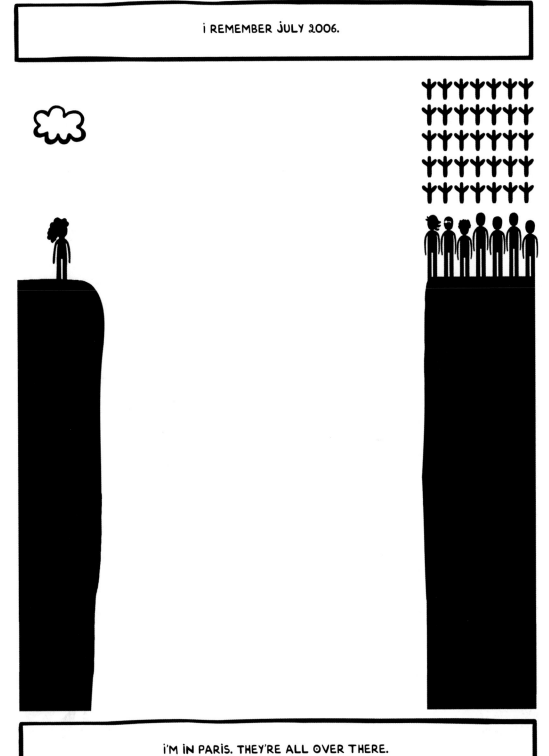

JUST TWENTY YEARS EARLIER, MY BIGGEST FEAR WAS LOSING THEM.

i made chicken with rice

your father listened to Mozart
all day long

your brother finished reading
"The World According to Garp"

Chucri gave us some gas

...TO REASSURE ME.

ABOUT THE AUTHOR

Zeina Abirached was born in Beirut in 1981 in the middle of the civil war and was ten years old when it finally ended. She studied graphic arts and commercial design at the Lebanese Academy of Fine Arts (ALBA) and in 2002 was awarded the top prize at the International Comic Book Festival in Beirut for her first graphic novel, *Beyrouth-Catharsis*. She moved to Paris in 2004, where she attended the National School of Decorative Arts. In 2006, she published her two graphic novels in French with the publisher Cambourakis, and the next year her short animated film, *Mouton* (*Sheep*), received a prize nomination during the 5th Tehran International Animation Festival.

While surfing a French online news archive, she came across a television documentary made in Beirut in 1984. The reporters were interviewing the residents of a street near the demarcation line that cut the city in two. A woman whose home had been hit by the bombings spoke a single sentence that startled her: "You know, I think maybe we're still more or less safe here."

That woman was her grandmother. At that moment, she knew she had to tell the story of their lives in Beirut.